Milkvetch
&
Violets

Poems by
Mohammad Reza Shafi'i-Kadkani

Selected & Translated by
Mojdeh Bahar

MAGE PUBLISHERS

Copyright © 2021 Mojdeh Bahar

All rights reserved. No part of this book may be reproduced or retransmitted in any manner whatsoever, except in the form of a review, without the written permission of the publisher.

Mage Publishers Inc
www.mage.com

Library of Congress Cataloging-in-Publication Data
Available at the Library of Congress

ISBN 978-1-949445-32-9

Email: as@mage.com •
Mage online: www.mage.com

For Tina

Contents

INTRODUCTION, *xi*
POEMS, 1
Mountain Osier, 2
  Beware…, 3
  Wild Garden, 4
  Which Anticipation…?, 5
  Safe Travels!, 6
  Query, 8
  Rain's Travelogue, 9
  Doubt, 10
  Migration of Violets, 11
  In the Presence of the Wind, 12
  Response, 13
  Languor, 14
  Sea, 15
  Clear Blue, 16
  Pen and Ink, 17
  A Prayer in Strait, 18
  Youth, 19
  Poppy's Life Story 1, 20
  Autumnal Climate, 21
  Poppy's Life Story 2, 22
  Tree's Psalm, 23

Hymn, 24
Mourning the Essence of the Storm, 25
January, 26
With the Rose Petal, 27
The Greenness of Moss, 28
Current Mood, 29
Before the Tree, 30
No Man's Land, 32
Inquiry 2, 33
Birdsong, 34
Sun's Makeup, 35
Leaf of Green Trees, 36
A Treeless Leaf, 38
Withstanding a Thorn, 39
A Journey in the Lily Pad, 40
Sunflower, 41
Floral Tile Design, 42
Compass, 43
Claw to Claw with Death, 44
Blowballs, 45
Cold Snap, 46

Toad's Admonition, 47
Poetry Therapy, 48
Missing, 49
In Search of that Everlasting Moment, 50
Wintersweet Flower, 51
Petunia's Trumpet, 52
Seed of the Heart, 53
In Fear of Drought, 54
Clock & Calendar, 55
Almond Blossom, 56
Blooming, 57
The Fruit of Death, 58

CHRONOLOGICAL LIST OF POEMS, 61
SOURCES, 69
Acknowledgements, 71

Introduction

Mohammad Reza Shafi'i-Kadkani is a contemporary Iranian poet, literary critic, editor, author and translator. Born in 1939, his childhood days were divided between the village of Kadkan and the city of Mashhad in northeastern Iran. He was educated in the religious tradition for his primary and secondary education. He later earned his doctorate in Persian literature from Tehran University where he teaches today.

My introduction to Kadkani's poetry was at fourteen when I had left Iran for Europe and then the United States. I received a letter from my best friend who was still living in Iran. The letter contained the poem "Safe Travels!" which is included in this selection and has since become internationally known. It's also been put into songs by various vocalists. Milkvetch and breeze have a dialog in this poem, where the shackled plant asks that the free breeze carry a message to the blossoms and the rain, after traversing a tough terrain. The poem resonated deeply with me as its symbolism spoke to our predicament: one of us had left while the other had stayed put. For my family, like many others, leaving Iran represented freedom of thought and expression. It represented hope. In reading more of Kadkani's poetry I learned that in his nature poetry he acknowledges hardships but either anticipates and solves the problem, hopes for its future resolution or in the case of the inevitable, cautions the blossoms to prevent deception and loss. His wildflowers and birds anticipate the arrival of spring. His milkvetch contemplates its predicament but finds a way to convey its message through the breeze. His wintersweet outsmarts the drought; his mountain osier, pine and petunia are the songs of life; his rain cleanses the earth and purifies the words; his poppy is reckless, his sea fearless; his jasmines and sweetbriars are miraculous.

Persian poetry spans a millennium. Rudaki, a tenth century poet, is often considered the first Persian poet. From tenth to early twentieth century, namely 1920s, poets composed classical poems. Classical Persian poetry in its many forms and meters is highly structured and well defined. In 1920, Nima Yooshij, finding the classical structures restrictive, introduced *she'r-e no* "new poetry" and Nima became the father of modern Persian poetry. Since then, new poetry and classical poetry have coexisted. While some poets compose modern or classical poetry exclusively, others compose both classical and modern poetry. Mohammad Reza Shafi'i Kadkani is one such poet.

Kadkani wrote his first poem at the age of seven. In his three collections, spanning six decades, one can find traditional poetic forms such as *ghazal* (ode or sonnet) and *charpareh* (couplets) as well as Nimaic poems (free verse). Shafi'i Kadkani is at once a modern poet and a classical poet, well versed in both traditions. His themes, language, and style are unique, fusing the old with the new, the classic with the modern. His vocabulary is incredibly rich and deceptively simple. The beauty of his poetry resides in the union of these dualities. Literary critics describe his poetry as at times social and at other times naturalist. His poetry seems to occupy an in between space both in form and substance. He, unlike many of his contemporaries, is a harbinger of hope.

This selection is largely focused on Kadkani's poetry about nature that demonstrates both the dualities and the in between space of his writing. His seasons are not ordinary seasons, they are not easily defined, they capture the transitions between fall and winter, and the anticipation of spring. His highly musical verses emphasize movement and change in nature, and his nature is filled with possibilities and hope.

About the Selection

In addition to many scholarly books and articles, Mohammad Reza Shafi'i-Kadkani has published three volumes of poetry, each volume containing multiple previously published collections (he also writes under the pen name M. Sereshk*). The first volume *A Mirror for Voices* (1997) contains seven collections, the second volume *The Second Millennium of the Mountain Deer* (1999) and the third volume *A Child Named Joy* (2020) each contains five collections.

This selection includes fifty-four poems chosen from the three volumes. Fifty of the poems explore themes through nature or natural elements generally; and plants, seasons, storms, and different forms of water specifically. Four of the poems, "Compass," "Missing," "Clock and Calendar, "and "Poetry Therapy," though not related to nature, are too beautiful to leave out.

---

* Pen names have long been used in Persian literature. They have been used as nouns, or subjects in a poem. They have also given poets an opportunity to comment on their own poetry or to use themselves as the interlocutor to indirectly convey a message to the reader. They can be chosen based on a variety of elements: the poet's birthplace, lineage, family traits, profession, as an homage to the poet's mentor, or as a shortened version of their name. Modern Persian poets have often chosen their pen names by using their first initial followed by a noun, for example: Mehdi Akhavan Sales's pen name is M. Omid; M (for his first initial) followed by Omid (hope); Ahmad Shamlou's pen name is A. Bamdad (morning); and Mohammad Reza Shafi'i Kadkani's pen name is M. Sereshk (tear, and also dew or rain). Interestingly, this nomenclature is limited to men. Although at times contemporary women poets have used a pseudonym in some of their poems, e.g. Simin Behbahani signs some of her poems as Kowli (Gypsy).

The poet has dated and indicated the location for only some of the poems. The dates are sometimes specific, and at other times only a month, year or a season is mentioned.

Poems

Mountain Osier*

Embraced by this ancient valley
On this silent, blind and deaf rock
The lonesome mountain osier
   peers proudly over the clouds.

Piercing the narrow bosom of the rock
With its roots searching for life
No fear of the sharp hatchet of lightning
Nor thoughts of the raging storm.

Where no cloud has caused rain
Where no passerby has passed
The lonesome mountain osier
   is the song of life, green and tall
   budding at the edge of the cliff.

Jul/Aug 1964
Kadkan

---

* [Poet's footnote]: Mountain Osier (Willow) is a wild willow, with narrow leaves, it is drought tolerant and grows in dry valleys or amid rocks.

Beware…

O branch of almond blossom!
Welcome–
Greetings!

You're smiling?
But
This indecent grove
  with this lonesome night...
Beware of this faint little breeze!
  this intermittent caress of time!

You laugh in vain, alas!
Press the foot of delay
  in the stirrup of silence.

Don't believe the cloud...
Don't believe the wind...
Don't believe the laughter of the morning sun...
I only know all these dyes and deceptions.

                                Feb/Mar 1965
                                Mashhad

Wild Garden

The neighbor's rooster was crowing,
The raindrops of a March dawn
   falling from a hurried cloud.

The fleeting clouds, in the blue morning sky
  —like a blowball* on a chicory field—
   flowing from the mountain and the desert.

And I, at the height of that Godly moment,
Deep in thought in the woods,
   whether on the other side of this garden of
   cloud flowers
   in that deep azure, there is someone
   for whom this garden is a greenhouse
   and the crystalline lantern of the star
   —in this enduring, vast royal blue sky—
   serves as the bright light of his house,
Or whether this garden,
   is wild, crawling and self-sustaining?

                                   Spring 1963
                                   Mashhad

---

* The fluffy seed ball of a dandelion. Also referred to as dandelion clock.

Which Anticipation…?

Sing, O titmouse, your song!
   —on that bare, flowerless, leafless branch—
   for you anticipate the arrival of spring.

But, with which anticipation shall I delight
   this despairing heart of mine
   —that's not fazed by a thing?

                                  Jan/Feb 1964
                                  Mashhad

Safe Travels!

"Where to, in such a rush?"
 the milkvetch* asked the breeze.

"I feel depressed here.
Don't you have the desire
 to leave this dusty desert?"

"I am all desire
Alas,
I am shackled here."

"Where to, in such a rush?"

"Anywhere, but here,
where I can feel at home."

---

* Many species of milkvetch grow in Iran, more than half of which are native plants. They are bushes with beautifully colored flowers. They grow in many parts of the country including the province of Khorasan, where the poet was born. In North America, some species of milkvetch are known as locoweed.

"Safe travels
But
For us and for God,
Once you have traversed this desert of dread,
Convey our regards![†]
To the blossoms, to the rain

[†] In 2015 this poem was inscribed on a wall in Clarensteeg in Leiden, Netherlands with an English translation by Dick Davis entitled "Travel Safely!"

Query

Suppose that this robust tree
  at the peak of maturity
  is impregnated by a sinful breeze;

But
—O grieving black cloaked cloud!—
What have these blossoms done
  to be left bruised and silent?

Suppose God did not want this garden
  to be caressed by the cloud or the wind,
What about these blossoms, wilted and
  damaged by the cold spring,
What had they done?

Feb/Mar 1965
Mashhad

Rain's Travelogue

The last page of rain's travelogue reads:
The earth is filthy.

Doubt

I said: "Spring has arrived."
You said: "Yet trees have no lofty thoughts of
  blooming.
As if the trees
  don't believe that this cloud,
  this breeze
  are the harbingers of that green truth."

"Indeed, spring is not a green robe
  that one can wear
  upon desire."

February 1967
Tehran

Migration of Violets

In late winter,
   the migration of nomadic violets
   is beautiful.

In the midday light, in March,
When enveloped in spring scented satin,
With root and soil
   —their portable home—
In small wooden boxes
Out of the cold shadows
   to street corners they are transported:

A stream of thousand chants resonate inside
   of me:
I wish...
I wish, like violets (in soil-filled boxes),
   one day, one could
   take one's homeland along to wherever
   one desired.
In light of rain
In pure sunlight.

                                       Feb/Mar 1967

In the Presence of the Wind

My words
I wash them in the stream of dawn;
My moments,
In the light of rain;
So I can write you an honest poem
So with no concern
No ambiguity,
And the wind as my witness,
My words
   —those of a nomad of plains & deserts—
   will assure you:
I love you to the brink of madness!

Jul/Aug 1967

Response

Do you know why, like the wave,
   as I redound, I am steadily reduced?
For on this opaque veil,
In this inner darkness,
What I want, I don't see,
&
What I see, I don't want.

                              Aug 2, 1967
                                Tehran

Languor

On a stream bank
I sit
Water flows.

All week,
Tired
I anticipate Friday.*
All day Friday
  in utter loneliness
  yet again
I anticipate Saturday and work...

I sit
Water flows.

Nov/Dec 1967

---

* In Iran, the work week is from Saturday to Thursday and Friday is a day of rest.

Sea

I don't envy the swamp's slumber
Asleep in the dead of night peacefully.
I am the sea, fearless of the storm:
The sea, forever sleeping fitfully.

1967
Tehran

Clear Blue

The fine moment
The pure moment.

The clear blue moment of a March morning,
The moment of floating clouds,
A moment, bright and
　deep & flowing
　　—the very essence of water.

A moment when your laughter
　delivered rapture to the fir,
The clear blue moment of the awakened
　garden,
The bright moment and the rare reunion.

July 5, 1968
Tehran

Pen and Ink

The dry hand of winter
  has stripped the garden of color
Astonished, you presume,
There has never been a garden nor a
  spring here.

1969
Tehran

A Prayer in Strait

From beyond spring and rain
From beyond tree and stream
From the farthest corners of the universe
Be my closest confidant!

There's no rooster's crow
No moonlight
No break of dawn.
Be the dawn of day
   in the lonely solitude of my night!

Jan 18,1970
Tehran

Youth

This red rose
This fresh red rose of a hundred petals
This red rose of the Gods' crowns
   whose petals you pluck everyday with
   hatred
   one by one
   —so not to witness others perceive its
   wilting—
In a few days its petals,
Will gradually disappear.

Feb 12, 1970
Tehran

Poppy's Life Story 1

What is the poppy's life story?

Shouldering a banner of blood at dawn,
The wind and its romantic aria,
Entrusting its life on the path of love,
   to the wind and que sera, sera.*

1971/72
Tehran

---

* While the correct expression *quel che sarà sarà* is Italian. A song, popularized in the 1950s by Doris Day, spelled the expression que sera, sera as if it were Spanish. This expression is now part of the English language, and many others.

Autumnal Climate

Behold the old chestnut tree, over there,
Half autumnal, half vernal:
As if the magic of fall
   has laboriously climbed up to its waist
And from there,
   could go no further.

Fall 1974
Tehran

Poppy's Life Story 2

O poppies of my springs!
My darlings!
Your blood shall not be expunged,
   from soil or stone,
Not even by Noah's flood
For it spreads forever more
The same way the rain,
   ever more rapidly
   renders the face of the Judas tree,
   lush and more rosy-cheeked than before.

Jan. 1975
Oxford

Tree's Psalm

I'd rather be a tree
   flogged by blizzard and thunder
   dynamically burgeoning and booming
Than a meek rock
   cuddled and caressed by rain
   silently listening.

>Dec. 1975
>Oxford

Hymn

> So dismiss the appearance from your mind
> Ibn Arabi*

I know you
Your eyes
The hosts of sunlight in spring dawn in the gardens.

I know you
Your words
The keys to our locks.

I know you
Creator and companion of light,
Your hands
A bridge to seeing God.

Dec. 16, 1975
Princeton

---

* Ibn Arabi is a Sufi mystic saint and poet. In the next phrase—which Kadkani has not included—Ibn Arabi continues, "and seek the essence to get to know it". One could simplify the quote to "forget the appearance, seek the essence, in order to know it."

Mourning the Essence of the Storm

Listen to the vocal cords of rain,
   in this sunset of springs!

This is not a poem, it's a curtain of blood
It's my destruction and yours.

It's the mutiny of meaning against sound,
   in the trachea of roaring thunder.

Words grinding their teeth
Mourning the essence of the storm.

1975/76

January

The pine's glorious green stature
  in the grove
  is an eternal God
  with an earful of rain's prayers.

Companions, in honor of the birth of soil's
  stepson
Do not break it, do not cut it down!

Jan. 1976
Tehran

With the Rose Petal

As raindrops
 never return to the sky,
with wounded feet
I will stay the course to the end of Fall.

Friends!
I vow to water,
I vow to mirror,
 to wipe the sorrow off the faces of the
 children of Neyshabur*
 with a rose petal.

1976
Princeton

---

* A city in Khorasan in northeastern Iran,
75 kilometers from the poet's birthplace, Kadkan.

The Greenness of Moss

The impudence of moss
   tricks the river that it is leaving
Yet it stays put
It's been years and years.

Many a time the river
   crimson at dawn
The greenness of moss
Still floating in the water
Pretends to leave
Yet it stays put.
It still remains.

The river ran off with the rock
But the greenness of moss
Pretends to leave, yet it stays put
Standing like a dragon.

It tricks the river
It's been years and years and years.

April 17, 1976
Oxford

Current Mood

Night fell and enveloped the day,
For dawn and morning it blocked the way

Too long in the bosom and notebook it remained,
Song, lyrics and poem all decayed.

Before the Tree

Early morning,
The garden brimming with spruce firs
   and songs.

Robins soaring
& soaring
Wings spread, in droves &
   droves
From the eastern horizon
The milky ray of dawn
   reflected in their gaze,
   in waves & waves & waves.

At twilight, every plant & leaflet
   would taste
   that green sound,
   —from the other side of the wall separating
   speech & sound—
The sound that Moses would hear from the
   tree.

Though I was rid of my self
   and set free

There, I remained a stranger & no one
   was aware of my presence.

I offered all my words
Yet the tree
   did not let me in, not even for a moment.

No Man's Land

I, along with the poem and the stream,
We went
And went,
We reached a place where
   there were no footsteps,
Nothing familiar.

Where trees were of a different kind,
Birds of a different flock.
A voice from afar,
The voice of God,
Free.

While flying,
   from one garden to another
Nobody would inspect
   the underwings of swallows,
   of butterflies,
The poppy
   would not be silenced by the storm
Its light always brightly shone.

I do not know where that was!
I do not know where that was!

Inquiry 2

If not by a miracle
How do you explain
   blooming in the dragon's breath
   countless white jasmines and red sweetbriers?

Birdsong

On a green boxwood branch
  a joyful little bird sings
—Nobody knows for it's
  a well-kept secret—
Maybe it sings out of joy
Maybe it's joyful because it sings!

Sun's Makeup

If sound were visible
What flowers
      What flowers
Could be picked from the garden of your
  voice
    with each song!

If only sound were visible...

                                           August 14, 1987

Leaf of Green Trees

> "Every one of its leaves is a notebook"*
> Sa'adi

The breeze leafs through
   the leaves of the white poplar
   in the radius of the yellow flower
And the sparrow, cleverly,
   learns from each leaf a different lesson:

That this garden used to be in a seed
And that seed in yet another seed
As long as the world has existed,
   this seed too has existed.

The breeze leafs through
   the leaves of the white poplar
   in the radius of the yellow flower
And the sparrow, cleverly,
   learns from each leaf a different lesson:

---

* The poem refers to a verse of a poem by Sa'adi, a thirteenth century Iranian poet. It can be translated as:
   The green leaves of trees before God,
      each leaf is a notebook with lessons by the creator

That the sparrow comes from an egg,
And that egg from the essence of the
    sparrow
And the sparrow is from the heart of the
    egg.

The breeze leafs through
    the leaves of the white poplar:
That the sea is from this river
    and this river from rain clouds
And the clouds are the progeny of the sea.

There is no breeze and the leaves of the
    white poplar
    no longer move
And the sparrow no longer learns any
    lessons,
Many questions occupy its mind
Remain unanswered
For it has not read any more books.

                                    1988/89

A Treeless Leaf
In reading Paul Celan[*]

If a tree becomes leafless in the fall,
Or numb due to the bitter cold
There is hope that the spring cloud
  will sprout its leaves as it brings relief.
The tree can live leafless
What's the grief?
Lament the condition of the treeless leaf!

Sept. 3, 1987

---

[*] Paul Celan is a Jewish Romanian-born poet, polyglot, translator and lecturer who wrote poems in Romanian and German. He was born in 1920 and drowned himself in the Seine in 1970. His life during the Holocaust was a major influence in his literary work. Survival (of a person as well as a language) and the importance of language are among the themes explored by Celan.

Withstanding a Thorn

Spring arrived and a leaf or fruit I had not
Like a cut branch, spring I had not

In this field, like tulip's center burnt to a coal,
I burned in secret and a spark I had not

The flower smiled at the branch and I ashamed of myself
For at springtime a leaf or fruit I had not

Flower! I lost you to a single taunt
The strength to withstand a thorn from your garden I had not

Not for a moment did my fortune lead me to your doorstep
For you, the value of a speck of dust, I had not.

A Journey in the Lily Pad

There are many skies
Skies the color of astonishment
Skies the color of olive
Skies the color of Neyshaburi turquoise
I travel through them all.

Dawn sky after spring showers,
Caspian sky mixed with clouds and
 verdigris
Moments of morning rays and daybreak.

Yet in the raindrop
On this lily
—Sorrow and joy interwoven
Like suffering and art—
One should note:
It's a different sky!

1989/90

Sunflower

Sunflower
And its prayer to the Sun
> At night
>> With clouds
>>> In the dark
Not for a moment loses
  its solar compass,
  stowed deep within its soul!

Floral Tile Design

The sparrow, throughout winter
        Longing
with such anticipation of garden and spring
  that she perceived the floral tile in the
  mosque,
        in January,
  as the dawn of spring

Compass

No guide, no map, no clear path

Two steps north
Two steps south
You who travels through this darkness
You blink and your opportunity is but ruin
   and collapse.

What do you deserve if not destitute?
For you sought everyone, everything,
   everywhere, but your own heart,
   your compass.

April 19, 1993

Claw to Claw with Death

Look at the cruel wind twist,
  to separate this branch from the leaf
Look at the leaf with its green love
  fight claw to claw with death.

April 29, 1993

Blowballs

Wind
  Crookedly
    Blows
       Here
       And a bunch of
            blowballs
                    Blow in from all sides
and
    their bushiness
bothers the eye and blocks the vision.

I am certain they bear false news
As there is a bounty of blowballs!

                        May 15, 1993

Cold Snap

After the long winter
  and
  the bitter cold
  cracking the mid-winter firn,*
This dogwood winter†
This suffering and silence
Will not endure.

---

* Firn is the intermediate stage between snow and ice.

† Dogwood winters are cold spells or short winter-like periods after the arrival of spring.

Toad's Admonition

Under thirst's attack in the blazing July sun
Shackled in scorching soil
The milkvetch laments:
"I spend my days noting the passage of time"

The toad in a cane thicket of slime and sludge
  responds:
"How long will you endure this thirst?
Liberate yourself like us,
Step forward, take a sip, shorten the rhyme"

The dry milkvetch bush says in response:
  "Hush!
Feet in shackles are more honorable than
  hands in slime"

April 10, 1976

Poetry Therapy

Every moment, with the slightest hint,*
I went in every direction
to find the possible hint of a cure
Alas, in *The Canon*,† I found no potion
but poetry
to salvage my soul.

---

* In the Persian text the word *Isharat* ("hints") is used which could indicate a reference to one of Avicenna's philosophical works, namely *Al-Isharat wa al-Tanbinat* (Remarks and Admonitions).

† *The Canon of Medicine* is a medical encyclopedia by Avicenna, 10-11th century philosopher and physician.

Missing

A child named Joy has long been missing
With bright light eyes
With hair as long as hope.

If you know of her whereabouts,
Contact us.
Here's our address:
At one end, Persian Gulf
At the other, Caspian Sea.

In Search of that Everlasting Moment

I leaf through petunia petals
I leaf through
  the years
  the days
I leaf through the sky
  the earth
I leaf through life
  openly and secretly
  in search of that everlasting moment.

Wintersweet Flower

The thought of blooming
  and recounting the love story,
The anticipation of spring
Billowed within wintersweet flower so
—as December's cold breath cracked the rock—
Before growing leaves,
It bloomed.

Petunia's Trumpet

In the age of howling death
In an exile where all melodies
   compose songs of destitution and demise
The petunias' trumpet
Is the call of life
Awaiting sunrise.

                                         March 25, 2009

Seed of the Heart

I hope one day,
I can plant my heart like a seed
   so that
Tomorrow
It'll bear fruit and the lovers' progeny
   will not become extinct from the earth
Can one persist, in this manner, I wonder?

In Fear of Drought

The young Judas tree has budded in our garden
   in mid-March
And all the buds it has had on its branch,
   today, it has opened them all.

◻

It, instinctively, has identified its enemy
And in fear of the impending drought
A month earlier
It has begun
   the uproar of blooming and recounting.

February-March 2009

Clock & Calendar

You noticed your hair in the mirror and
   surrendered to fear
Yet the one who still adores you
   despises clocks & calendars.

Almond Blossom

Blessed is the March dawn
  when the earth reverts to its infancy
  to nurse on the nectar of the almond blossom.

Blooming

Sprouting out of the heart of this rock, in the
 bitter cold
 joyfully, magnificently and patiently
O wildflower! for the glory of God
What words can one use to thank you
 sufficiently?

The Fruit of Death

The seed of silence
  grew roots and
  leaves,
  a thousand branches
  and
Bore the fruit of death.

Chronological List of Poems

What follows is the name of the collection or volume, the date and place of each poem, when indicated by the poet. The list has been organized chronologically. In cases where the poems are not dated, the date of publication of the collection or volume has been used. The natural elements present in each poem also have been listed.

WILD GARDEN
Wake Up Song, pp. 25–6, spring 1963, Mashhad.
Garden, chicory, blowball.

WHICH ANTICIPATION...?
Wake Up Song, p. 45, Jan/Feb 1964, Mashhad.
Titmouse, spring, branch.

MOUNTAIN OSIER
Wake Up Song, pp. 53–54, July/Aug 1964, Kadkan.
Mountain osier (willow), mountain, lightening, storm.

BEWARE...
Wake Up Song, pp. 73–4, Feb/March 1965, Mashhad.
Almond blossom, grove, breeze, cloud, sun, wind.

Query
Wake Up Song, pp. 75–6, Feb/March 1965, Mashhad.
Tree, breeze, branch of blossoms, spring, wind, cloud.

Withstanding a Thorn
Whispers, p. 70, 1965/66; no date (for the poem), no place.
Spring, fruit, leaf, branch, garden, tulip, thorn.

Doubt
Like a Tree on a Rainy Night, pp. 50–1, Feb 1967, Tehran.
Spring, trees, breeze, cloud.

Migration of Violets
As the Leaf Would Say, pp. 22–3, Feb/March 1967, no place.
Violets, spring, winter.

In the Presence of the Wind
As the Leaf Would Say, pp. 50–1, July/Aug 1967, no place.
Stream, dawn, rain, wind.

Response
In the Back Alleys of Neyshabur, p. 70, Aug 2, 1967, Tehran
Wave, sea.

Languor
As the Leaf Would Say, pp. 63–4, Nov/Dec 1967, no place
Stream, water.

Sea
In the Back Alleys of Neyshabur, p. 39, 1967, Tehran
Sea, storm, swamp.

Clear Blue
Like a Tree on a Rainy Night, pp. 32–3, July 5, 1968, Tehran.
Fir, garden.

Rain's Travelogue
As the Leaf Would Say, p. 17, collection published in 1968/69, no date (for the poem), no place.
Rain, earth.

Black and White Drawing
Traces of Sorrow, p. 100, 1969, Tehran.
Winter, spring, garden.

A Prayer in Strait
Like a Tree on a Rainy Night, p. 17, Jan 18, 1970, Tehran.
Spring, rain, tree, stream, moonlight, dawn.

Youth
Like a Tree on a Rainy Night, p. 47, February 12, 1970, Tehran.
Red rose.

Safe Travels!
In the Back Alleys of Neyshabur, pp. 15–6, collection published in 1971/72, no date (for the poem), no place.
Milkvetch, desert, blossoms, rain, breeze.

POPPY'S LIFE STORY 1
Of Being and Composing, p. 57, 1971/2, Tehran.
Poppy, dawn, wind.

AUTUMNAL CLIMATE
Like a Tree on a Rainy Night, p. 60, Fall 1974, Tehran.
Chestnut tree, fall, spring.

POPPY'S LIFE STORY 2
Of Being and Composing, pp. 58–9, January 1975, Oxford.
Poppy, Judas tree, spring.

HYMN
Like a Tree on a Rainy Night, pp. 36–7, December 16, 1975, Princeton.
Sunlight, spring, garden.

TREE'S PSALM
Of Being and Composing, pp. 55, December 1975, Oxford.
Tree, rain, thunder, blizzard.

MOURNING THE ESSENCE OF THE STORM
Traces of Sorrow, p. 106, 1975/6, no place.
Sunset, storm, thunder, spring.

JANUARY
Like a Tree on a Rainy Night, p. 53, January 1976, Tehran.
Pine, rain.

TOAD'S ADMONITION
In Praise of Doves, pp. 18–9, April 10, 1976, no place.
Milkvetch.

THE GREENNESS OF MOSS

Traces of Sorrow, pp. 21–2, April 17, 1976, Oxford.
Moss, river, water, rock, greenness.

With the Rose Petal
Traces of Sorrow, p. 101, 1976, Princeton.
Raindrops, sky, fall, water, rose petal.

Before the Tree
The Scent of Moulian River, pp. 68–9, collection published in 1978/79, no date (for the poem), no place.
Spruce, robin, dawn, plant, leaflet, tree.

No Man's Land
The Scent of Moulian River, pp. 75–6, collection published in 1978/79, no date (for the poem), no place.
River, trees, birds, butterflies, swallow.

Current Mood
The Scent of Moulian River, p. 55, collection published in 1978-79, no date (for the poem), no place.
Night, dawn, morning.

Inquiry 2
The Scent of Moulian River, p. 52, collection published in 1978-79, no date (for the poem), no place.
White jasmines, red sweetbriars (dog roses).

Cold Snap
Traces of Sorrow, p. 61, March/April 1979, no place.
Winter, firn, dogwood winter.

Sun's Makeup

An Ode to Sunflower, p. 21, Aug 14, 1987, no place.
Sun, flower, garden.

A TREELESS LEAF
An Ode to Sunflower, p. 65, Sept 3, 1987, no place.
Tree, leaf, cloud, fall, spring

LEAF OF GREEN TREES
The Comet, pp. 59–61, 1988-89, no place.
Breeze, sparrow, garden, seed, white poplar.

A JOURNEY IN THE LILY PAD
An Ode to Sunflower, pp. 71–72, 1989, no place.
Sky, spring, dawn, lily.

COMPASS★
Traces of Sorrow, pp. 80–1, April 19, 1993, no place.

CLAW TO CLAW WITH DEATH
A Child Named Joy, p. 162, April 29, 1993, no place.
Wind, leaf, branch

BLOWBALLS
Traces of Sorrow, pp. 55–6, May 15, 1993, no place.
Blowball, wind.

BIRDSONG
An Ode to Sunflower, p. 20, volume published in 1997, no date (for the poem), no place.
Boxwood, bird.

SUNFLOWER
An Ode to Sunflower, p. 88, volume published in 1997, no date (for the poem), no place.
Sunflower, sun, clouds.

FLORAL TILE DESIGN
Traces of Sorrow, p. 49, volume published in 1997, no date (for the poem), no place.
Sparrow, flower, spring, winter.

IN FEAR OF DROUGHT
A Child Named Joy, p. 156, Feb/March 2009, no place.
Judas tree.

BLOOMING
A Child Named Joy, p. 287, March 25, 2009, no place.
Wildflower, winter.

PETUNIA'S TRUMPET
A Child Named Joy, p. 288, March 25, 2009, no place.
Petunia, sun.

POETRY THERAPY★
A Child Named Joy, p. 238, volume published in 2020, no date (for the poem), no place.

MISSING★
A Child Named Joy, p. 39, volume published in 2020, no date (for the poem), no place.

IN SEARCH OF THAT EVERLASTING MOMENT
A Child Named Joy, p. 150, volume published in 2020, no date (for the poem), no place.
Petunia, sky.

Wintersweet Flower
A Child Named Joy, p. 312, volume published in 2020, no date (for the poem), no place.
Wintersweet flower.

Seed of the Heart
A Child Named Joy, p. 404, volume published in 2020, no date (for the poem), no place.
Seed, fruit.

Clock and Calendar★
A Child Named Joy, p. 370, volume published in 2020, no date (for the poem), no place.

Almond Blossom
A Child Named Joy, p. 324, volume published in 2020, no date (for the poem), no place.
Almond blossom, nectar.

The Fruit of Death
A Child Named Joy, p. 155, volume published in 2020, no date (for the poem), no place.
Seed, roots, branch, fruit.

★Poems with no elements of nature

Sources Used

In translating the poems contained in the first two volumes, *A Mirror for Voices* and *The Second Millennium of the Mountain Deer*, the individual collections in each volume were used. *A Mirror for Voices* includes seven collections: *Whispers, Wake Up Song, As the Leaf Would Say, In the Back Alleys of Neyshabur, Like a Tree on a Rainy Night, Of Being and Composing and the Scent of Moulian River.* The Second *Millennium of the Mountain Deer* encompasses five collections: *An Ode to Sunflower, In Praise of Doves, The Comet, Elegy for Koshmar Cypress*, and *Traces of Sorrow*. In translating the poems that appear in the most recent volume, *A Child Named Joy,* the compilation itself has been used.

COMMENTARIES ON KADKANI AND HIS POETRY

Abbassi, H., ed. *Safarnameh-ye Baran* [Rain's Travelogue] (Tehran: Sokhan, 2009).

Bashardoost, Mojtaba. *Dar Josteju-ye Neyshabur* [In Search of Neyshabur](Tehran: Saless, 2007):

Sharifi, F. *Shafi'i Kadkani*, (Tehran: Negah, 2015).

POETRY EDITIONS

Shafi'i Kadkani, M.R., *Zemzemeha* [Whispers] (Tehran: Sokhan, 2009): 70.

———. *Shabkhuni* [Wake Up Song] (Tehran: Sokhan, 2009): 25, 26, 45, 53, 54, 73, 74, 75, 76.

———. (2009). *Az Zaban-e Barg* [As the Leaf Would Say] (Tehran: Sokhan, 2009): 17, 22, 23, 50, 51,63, 64.

———. *Dar Koocheh Baghha-ye Neyshabur* [In the Back Alleys of Neyshabur] (Tehran: Sokhan, 2009): 15, 16, 39, 70.

———. *Mesl-e Derakht dar Shab-e Baran* [Like a Tree on a Rainy Night] (Tehran: Sokhan, 2009): 17, 32, 33, 36, 37, 47, 50, 51, 53, 60.

———. *Az Boodan-o Sorudan* [Of Being and Composing]. (Tehran: Sokhan, 2009): 55, 57, 58, 59.

———. *Boo-ye Ju-ye Muliyan* [The Scent of Muliyan River] (Tehran: Sokhan, 2009): 52,55, 68, 69, 75, 76.

———. *Khati ze Deltangi* [Traces of Sorrow]. (Tehran: Sokhan, 2009): 21, 22, 49, 55, 56, 61, 80, 81, 100, 101, 106.

———. *Ghazali Bara-ye Gol-e Aftabgardan* [An Ode to Sunflower] (Tehran: Sokhan, 2009): 20, 21, 65, 71,72, 88.

———. *Setareh Donbalehdar* [The Comet] (Tehran: Sokhan, 2009): 59, 60, 61.

———. *Dar Setayesh-e Kabutarha* [In Praise of Doves](Tehran: Sokhan, 2009): 18, 19.

———.*Tefli be Nam-e Shadi* [A Child Named Joy] (Tehran: Sokhan, 2020): 39, 150, 155, 156, 238, 287, 288, 312, 324, 370, 404.

Acknowledgments

I initially started this project to share a single poem with my daughter, Tina, and then went on to translate the second poem and the third and.... She has been my cheerleader, my first reader, the most caring critic and editor as well as my inspiration.

I would like to thank Glenna Elisabeth Thomas for the drawings; Karen Odden, Sue Ano, Sayeh Eghtesadinia, Arjang Assad, and Hadi Bahar for helping me find the most precise words at all hours, and for their love and encouragement.

Other Mage Poetry Titles

Faces of Love: Hafez and the Poets of Shiraz
Bilingual Edition / Translated by Dick Davis

*The Mirror of My Heart:
A Thousand Years of Persian Poetry by Women*
Bilingual Edition / Translated by Dick Davis

Layli and Majnun
Nezami Ganjavi / Translated by Dick Davis

Vis and Ramin
Fakhraddin Gorgani / Translated by Dick Davis

Shahnameh: The Persian Book of Kings
Abolqasem Ferdowsi / Translated by Dick Davis

Rostam: Tales of Love and War from Persia's Book of Kings
Abolqasem Ferdowsi / Translated by Dick Davis

Borrowed Ware: Medieval Persian Epigrams
Introduced and Translated by Dick Davis

When They Broke Down the Door: Poems
Fatemeh Shams / Introduction and translations by Dick Davis

Pearls That Soak My Dress: Elegies for a Child
Jahan Malek Khatun / translated by Dick Davis

Another Birth and Other Poems
By Forugh Farrokhzad, translated by Hasan Javadi
and Susan Sallée / Bilingual edition

Obeyd-e Zakani: Ethics of Aristocrats and other Satirical Works
translated by Hasan Javadi

Audio Books

Faces of Love: Hafez and the Poets of Shiraz
Translated by Dick Davis / Penguin Audio / Read by
Dick Davis, Tala Ashe and Ramiz Monsef

*The Mirror of My Heart:
A Thousand Years of Persian Poetry by Women*
Translated by Dick Davis / Penguin Audio / Read by
Dick Davis, Mozhan Marno, Tala Ashe and Serena Manteghi

Layli and Majnun
Nezami Ganjavi / Translated by Dick Davis
Penguin Audio / Read by
Dick Davis, Peter Ganim, Serena Manteghi and Sean Rohani

Vis and Ramin
Fakhraddin Gorgani / Translated by Dick Davis
Mage Audio / Read by
Mary Sarah Agliotta, Dick Davis (introduction)

My Uncle Napoleon
Iraj Pezeshkzad / Translated by Dick Davis
Mage Audio / Read by
Moti Margolin, Dick Davis (introduction)

Savushun: A Novel about Modern Iran
Simin Daneshvar / Translated by M.R. Ghanoonparvar
Mage Audio / Read by
Mary Sarah Agliotta, Brian Spooner (introduction)

Crowning Anguish: Taj al-Saltana
Memoirs of a Persian Princess
from the Harem to Modernity, 1884–1914
Introduction by Abbas Amanat / Translated by Anna Vanzan
Mage Audio / Read by
Kathreen Khavari

www.ingramcontent.com/pod-product-compliance
Lightning Source LLC
Chambersburg PA
CBHW031421160426
43196CB00008B/1012